Wild Riverbanks

Wild Riverbanks

ESSAYS & POEMS

Atalina Wright

Metadata

Names: Wright, Atalina – author
Title: Wild Riverbanks / Atalina Wright
Description: Nature writing, poetry, essays & memoirs

Classifications

Main – Nature and the Natural World, General Interest (WN)
Earth Energies (VXK) Poetry – by Individual Poets (DCF) / Memoir (BM)

Identifiers

Hardcover — 9781399907415

A Special Note

The interior design of this book was lovingly considered, assisting those readers who may need a little more space around the words and a slightly bigger font on the page.

Please also note that the meditations and adventures shared in Wild Riverbanks were based on the author's personal experiences, and do not constitute medical or fitness advice. No liability is accepted for any reader who embarks upon their own wild and wonderful adventures, or marvellous inner journeys, after reading this nature-inspired book. Although, the author does wish the reader tremendous fun, joy, and wellness in this regard!

To my children and grandchildren:
May you always remember our joyful adventures along
wild riverbanks.

You are loved!

Contents

She is the rose in my heart.

A (Fairly) Wild Introduction

From hiking through the crisp mountain valleys of the Lake District to wild swimming in waterfalls beloved by poets of old to silent meditations at sunrise, discovering wildflowers, and enjoying waterside adventures, *Wild Riverbanks* is a collection of personal essays, memoirs, and poetry, inspired by the rivers that I have frequented throughout the years, from my childhood to the present day.

This book is my gift to all those who carry a love of rivers, nature, and Mother Earth in their hearts and bones. It was also written for those of you who long to dip your toes into fresh waters, to feel the tall greying grass slip through your fingers and the gentle morning sun upon your skin, but are *unnaturally* estranged.

As you read, may you hear the tiny footsteps of wild animals scampering across the woodland floor and the serenity of the white swan gliding across the water. May you breathe the breathy joy of the mountain summit. May you enjoy unexpected encounters, humorous (true) tales, and emerge, as I, a little wiser and knowledgeable about the riverbanks in this book, than when you set off on your adventures.

Complimenting this book are my new *Wild Riverbanks* photography galleries, which you can view at www.atalinawright.com. Although one's actual presence and senses, when sat at the foot of England's longest waterfall (see Arctic Wildflowers) or when running from humping cows (see Randy Bullocks) can never truly be replicated with a photograph alone, they are nevertheless great visionary tools for our imaginations! And so, by the powers of creative alchemy—photographs and words combined—I hope that some chapters will spring to life and teleport you into nature for a while. There are also handy page references on the web galleries. The *reasonably* rare river pancakes are interesting ones to start with, I think.

As an added gift, I have written two simple meditation/relaxation exercises; you will find them in the final pages. One of my greatest joys is inspiring others to explore their intimate connection to the elements, and Mother Earth's wellness-enhancing wonders!

A vast, untarnished, and blossoming wilderness dwells inside us all. Of this, I am certain.

Stay wild and *naturally* wonderful!

Love always,

Atalina

By the water and beneath the trees,
I sit and listen and observe,
I feel and I witness …
Until the 'I' dissolves and there is only oneness.

Notes on the Tees

The River Tees begins its journey as it rises on the eastern slopes of Cross Fell in the North Pennines and passes through Cow Green reservoir (the highest in England), windy moorland, and the impressive falls of Cauldron Snout. It flows through a mineral-rich dale of quartz-dolerite (Whinstone) and moves into softer carboniferous limestone as it meets the equally glacial in origin, though perhaps more dramatic, 70 ft (21.34 meters) High Force waterfall, and its divine counterpart aptly named Low Force. From here the Tees bounces on and around the ancient town of Barnard Castle with its castle ruins still standing atop its lofty riverbanks, and the village of Whorlton and once popular, Whorlton Lido; a series of horseshoe-shaped golden waterfalls, and the home of many happy childhood memories from the '60s to the '90s (my vague recollections included), but long since closed off by landowners. And arrives at picturesque Winston, Gainford, and Darlington, before it scoops around the cobbled high street of Yarm and my former home Eaglescliffe in the borough of Stockton-on-Tees. Beyond here the river flows steadily towards the coast—a total of 137 km (85 miles) and into the icy waves of the North Sea. It also serves as a boundary between the city of Durham and North Yorkshire and has several tributaries; River Greta, River Lune, River Balder, River Leven, and River Skerne.

The River Tees is renowned for its industrial connections, and to historians for its Viking links. It has many adjoining becks, and the word 'beck' is derived from the Norse word 'bekkr'. The first Viking helmet (almost intact) was found in Yarm and is now housed at Preston Park Museum, Eaglescliffe—the grounds of which are featured in this book.

Rarely do we learn of the river's beauty—stunning, powerful, and curvaceous waters, teaming with abundant wildflowers, wildlife, waterfalls, and wild swimming spots!

I fell in love with the River Tees when I was a tiny welly-wearing paddler. She has been with me ever since.

To live a life on Earth is the ultimate adventure ...
Those who choose to come here
Are some of the bravest of the brave!

It began by the river ...

I am by the river, and I am mesmerized by the light. I observe how she moves. The water is in my veins. The trees are in my lungs. The winds are whispering. Nature is alive and talking ...

She knows me, *somehow.*

It's the '80s. I am here during the school holidays and every summer. Sometimes my grandparents sit nearby in their wide-striped wooden deckchairs and watch us swim and paddle. Nana is immaculately dressed, even on the riverbank. She is our caravan's captainess. Grandad loves darts and is skilled at making things from wood including the fences of his beautiful gardens. I'm with my younger sister, Losalia. There is only a couple of years between us. We play together, argue a little over who is going to sleep where and make tents out of blankets and parasols. Our French friend calls them 'tints,' and we like that. We also like to eat picnics; paste sandwiches, small tomatoes, crisps that you can shake your salt into, and mini-cookies—along woodland trails or by the river, or in the 'tint' on the grass outside our van. We *both* have an eye for adventure. Though neither of us are keen on the swooping bats on the bottom field. At dusk, they go for long brown wavy hair.

I like to follow the birds flying low across the rich frothy river waves, and I like to wonder … I drift out of thought and into imagination … I ponder a lot for a young person, I won't realise this until I am older.

I don't feel like I fit in much in the outside world. The stars are more familiar and the forests and rivers. I'm shy and awkward as I grow. My feet are long, and my ankles are skinny. I wear shoes with extra-thick T-straps for school, which I find quite ugly. But I love the hand-me-down river shorts, ripped and rugged—a gift from my older cousins, Damon and Mark. And I'm not sure why I feel so peaceful here, by the river, but I am. I sense the water flowing through the green valley landscape … I hear the rumbling of the waterfalls inside my body as if we are one. I feel the deep pulse of the Earth's heartbeat as my own—throbbing in my chest.

I know her, *somehow* …

My father was a handsome man, dark-haired and bright blue-eyed—exotic for an Englishman. He met my stunning Samoan mother in New Zealand. My mother was brave enough to leave everything behind and begin a new family life in the English countryside. If she had not been so courageous and travelled across half the world and the ocean, I never would have known the beauty of English rivers, and this book would have never been written.

I was eight-years-old and my sister was six when our father left this Earth suddenly and returned to the stars. He was thirty-three. I found great comfort by the River Tees. No one knew it but me. The waters washed away my tears, eased my aches and fears, and softened the uncomfortable lump in my throat. And though unfathomable, brought many days of joy thereafter. I stayed close to the river and her cleansing waters. Her wild yet familiar riverbanks welcomed me back every time.

Some of my earliest memories of the River Tees.

Age—
like Mother Nature, forgiveness, and love,
is a gift.

Thank Goodness for the Wild Folk

The wanderers still wander … The wanderers and wild folk … The tree-huggers and wellington wearers … The thinkers and readers … The walking stick lovers and the bramble pickers … The gardeners and countryside dwellers … The creators and dreamers … The sacred lovers and free-spirit believers … The solitude enthusiasts and meditators … The planet healers and new Earth weavers … The happiness-chasing children and wilderness achievers … Where the sun kisses the soils and the rivers glisten gladly.

Thank goodness for the wild folks!

Gingernuts and Carnation Milk

I was always a silent observer … I noticed the details: the steep wooden steps up the garden bank by the pansies, and the pale pink roses against the smooth but bobbly wood of the handmade round-edged branch fence, the aroma of the coffee and carnation milk with three gingernuts each morning, and bacon (I became a vegetarian in my mid-twenties) and large mushrooms with their storks carefully plucked out, fried in lard (popular with older generations back in the day), and the not-so-steady steel caravan steps, the need-to-be-emptied-often loo with blue hygienic water, the old heavy *iron* iron in the tiny cloakroom behind the curtain, the neat cooker and the Perspex fronted shelves above, the thick fabric semi-circular seating area with board games and blankets hidden beneath, the wood/steel spinning ashtrays, the big gas bottles and large water container hooked up outside, the canoe stored behind the white plastic netting underneath the van, the buckets and the fishing nets, and the miniature wooden toolkit. This was our caravan perched atop a riverbank. Caravans in the 1980s were comfortable enough for a few adults and a few children to live contentedly for several weeks. But *this* caravan was no ordinary caravan, for the views from its windows were of the River Tees! We awakened to the sounds of the valley and the river flowing faithfully below. In the wind and rain—in our little tin home from home—tiny gongs of elemental drummers echoed through the roof. And on sunny days, after breakfast, we'd pull up our socks and pull on our old pumps, wellies or jelly shoes and head off down to the river for an adventure or two.

Love sometimes shows up in the shape of a gingernut!

Along the bottom field, down the path, and then upstream, we often searched for tadpoles. We would put a few in our blue bucket and after a good ogle or after they had sprouted legs, returned them to the river.

Once, my sister and I found an old burnt caravan in the trees, behind the park, overlooking the river. We weren't supposed to play near it, so naturally, we went often. It was creepy; the discarded remnants of someone's life were left inside. We decided jointly that it was haunted, though we never had any *hard* evidence.

One day, as we were playing with a ball, it bounced away from that same park, through the fence and down toward the river. That was the day I discovered I was adventurous, *really* adventurous. I climbed down the vertical riverbank and discovered a hidden waterfall, enclosed by the most delicate wildflowers. I remember thinking: *This is so beautiful … fairies must live here!* And to this day, I still believe this to be true. This was my youthful response to the wonder that I felt. I'm not certain of my exact age, but I was young enough to get a telling off if I had been caught. My sister didn't tell. I still love her to this day.

The wild was in my bones and I knew it, even then.

We learned at a young age to be respectful of the river *and* its power—many flip flops had drifted off (friends, not my own), without any hope of return. We'd heard whispers, too, of folk being caught in the rapids downstream. Every so often, the rubber safety ring and rope was ripped from its wooden box and flung into the currents. Fast-moving waters were (rightly so) forbidden until our older years. By then, we knew the safe parts, the slippery parts, and the deep parts; the places to avoid. *This* was our outdoor education; instinctive skills that can only be learned in the wild.

As an awkward pre-teen, I followed the older kids (mainly boys) up to the bridge. A long rope and bit of wood had been tied at its centre. It was popular with adventurous adults and adolescents alike. The water was warm that day, without any strong currents, and deep enough to jump in (demonstrated by the others before me). I climbed the old stones of the bridge, took hold of the rope, grasped the wood, felt the adrenaline, and swung out ... The smooth cappuccino waters caught me gracefully. I remember the rush and the bubbles ... My arms reaching up, my legs kicking furiously, and my lips tasting the fresh air above. This was the river I loved—that I had come to appreciate every inch of, and to trust.

Not all youthful nature lovers are reckless.
Though it is prudent, perhaps, to teach them the ways of
the wild when they are young.

Tropical Riverbanks

I once fell backwards off a large rubber boat while white water rafting in the Caribbean. A giant hand plucked me out and plonked me back down on the bouncing seat, like a yoyo. I'm sure that for him; an experienced, tall, muscular, safety-focused boat captain—passengers like me; excitable, awe-eyed, buoyant-bottomed, were a frequent nuisance. Each time that we hit one of the rapids and sped around the small canyon of rocks, I levitated (impressively) several inches; my seat was the tubular inflated edge near the back of the large dingy. A spontaneous dip seemed inevitable … I was catapulted in back-flip fashion into tropical waters. The river was warm, the air sun-soaked, the life jacket and hard hat, well-fitted. I would have stayed in longer, but the captain had other ideas, and numerous other passengers, eager to continue with their adventure to attend to.

The second tropical waterways that I have swum in (a series of twelve out of twenty-seven cascading waterfalls, canyons, water chutes, and plunge pools) are hidden in the rainforest near Puerto Plata, Damajagua. Arriving by safari monster truck, and with an experienced guide, I made the steady hike up through the Septentrional Cordillera mountain range with my partner. Upon descent, each majestic pool was reached in succession by a combination of scrambling, swimming, jumping, climbing, and sliding. A final slide into a turquoise-tinted pool awaited. All enclosed by exotic forest.

But perhaps the most *striking* Caribbean waters with whom I enjoyed a stimulating encounter are Dunn's River Falls in Jamaica; multiple tiers of water elegantly washing down over cascades of silken bedrock. Powered by a phenomenal geochemical process, these falls continually regenerate and rebuild themselves from the spring water of travertine (limestone) deposits deeper therein. This waterfall is completely self-sufficient! And it is one of the few in the world that flow straight into the sea. The 180 ft (54.86 meters) high and 600 ft (182.88 meters) long falls descend like flowing white stairs—eventually reaching the soft pale sands and blue-green waters of the Caribbean Sea. Its only *small* downside is that its unique beauty and features make it one of the most popular tourist attractions on the island and Earth, with boatloads and coachloads of people arriving continuously, ready for the ultimate watery climb.

Newly married in the sweltering heat on a private beach in Negril days earlier (accompanied by a few of our family and friends), my husband and I arrived at the falls to the thrilling beats of reggae music booming through high-hanging speakers. There were smiles all around from visitors and excitement was palpable in the humid air. Dunn's River waterfall is climbed in groups by linking hand-to-hand with other people; the goal is to help each other up and to avoid slipping in or down. A man or woman with decent upper-arm muscles on either side of you is advantageous. Essentially, we spent our honeymoon in a human chain with strangers—trekking and dunking and splashing—in one of the world's most incredible waterfalls.

Jamaican water is cool and refreshing (especially in the steady heat of a Caribbean winter), and the vibes and Jamaicans, dare I say, far cooler. 'Yeah man, *no problem!*' is the response you are most likely to receive when asking for assistance. And despite the touristy atmosphere, and with a no-novice-left-behind attitude, a sense of unity and shared gratitude was gained as we reached the top.

English rivers are not *that* different to tropical rivers and riverbanks. We have the pools, chutes, and cascades … Not forgetting the occasional extraordinary sighting of those furry-faced water architects, otherwise known as otters. All that is missing are the monkeys, tropical air, and the effortlessly cool-vibe, Bob Marley-blasting, groovy, happy, river guides. But with our increasingly warm summers, there is still hope for us yet!

Old Cameras

In my twenties I would spend hours with an old (real) camera in my hands. I don't remember the name of the well-used black and white film camera the college tutor had loaned me, and that made me feel for the briefest of moments like a *real* photographer. Afterwards, I progressed to a sturdy Panasonic Lumix bridge—a sort of professional camera with stabilizers. Having been taught in the previous weeks how to process film in the darkroom, wielding skills that Ansel Adams had mastered, I went out into the wild, solo, to search for my first artistic subjects and things that had a silent voice; form, shadow, texture, and light—the magic ingredients of an interesting image. I'd spend hours wandering like a nomad, my solitude strangely comforted by the presence of a lens dangling from a thick black strap around my neck. I would photograph old buildings, wildflowers, boating enclosures at high tide, graffiti-covered walls, fruit seeds, shells on the sand, the ocean and its reliable show of unique waves, sunsets and sunrises, and sometimes people—wrinkles in the moonlight, smokers in their warm woollen coats taking the last drag before bedtime. Things of striking contrast, things of striking beauty, things of curiosity and strange interest. I would photograph the woods; micro shots of the tiniest plants growing in obscure spaces. Life thriving in unusual places. Peering into the ordinary and overlooked, to find extraordinary treasure.

The delicate details of nature always drew me in most ardently; the intricate and perfect design of leaves, petals, and trees; the seasons—watching how summer's riot of glorious colour shifted slowly into the softer simplicity of autumn and the stark silhouettes of winter. Spring always came. Spring, with its silent stirrings of renewed possibility; and the inner strength of a thousand oceans—breaking through and rising towards the new dawn. Emerging from its myriad of winter dwellings—always different from the year before. Sometimes, the blossom tree bloomed early, sometimes late, but the buds always carried the same layers of perfectly crafted colour. Of course, they never lasted long. A russet show of leaves was never far behind.

That's the thing about the seasons and wild riverbanks—
there are always new views to enjoy. The trees grow a little
taller and bushier. New wildflowers make their debut. The
rock pools move and shift with the tides of the water.
Nature's glorious show is forever changing.

Take me back to where the waters of my heart lay still. Where the glorious green trees rise and meet the sky. Let me sit for a while and drink the clean air and find myself in the place I never left. Take me to the rocks where I may dust off and mend my broken wings, and see again the world through enlightened eyes. Let me hear the pulsing heartbeat of the Earth as my own, and the ancient star songs the trees and water sing.

Summer Encounters

With my three children (then four, six, and eleven-years-old), I arrived at the river by the natural stone pool. A wavy-haired man, also with his children, was sat in *our* spot, dangling his lean legs in the water. Unexpectedly distracted, I did what many women who are fresh from the bowels of divorce do, I tried to ignore him! I was concerned that the words—*newly released back into the wild*—were etched delicately upon my forehead. Unprepared and unskilled in the art of making a good first impression with the male sex, I dumped my backpack roughly on the stones behind him and joined my eager-to-get-swimming children. I then stiffly edged my neoprene-clad bottom into a narrow waterfall and watched as they splashed into the water. I did my best *not* to stare at the handsome man, but it was difficult. We exchanged a few pleasant glances. He seemed familiar … and I wondered if we had played together as children, many years ago. A possibility that became more likely, when he commented that he also (somewhat vaguely) remembered coming to the river as a child. My son, Phoenix, who had slipped into Tarzan mode—excitedly beating on his chest, jumped off the rocks and into the pool—the perfect distraction. The man laughed along, and the River Tees proved once again, that you never know what delightful and unexpected gifts it may have to offer. My youngest daughter, Amaya, was in the waterfall beside me—still perfecting her river wings. My eldest, Latalia, was off exploring independently, as all young women eventually desire to do. After a short while, the boys, his (handsome man's) and mine, started mucking around like old-new friends—a lovely thing that happens when children meet waterside; mutual excitement, feral tendencies, and keen-eyes for adventure. If only I hadn't poured myself into a tiny wetsuit, which had restricted my physical movements by at least thirty percent—I'd have been able to breathe freely and frolic flirtatiously in the water beside them!

Despite my wetsuit handicap, my children were comfortably suited and equipped with two paddle boards— a worthwhile investment from a previous seaside trip. And it wasn't long, on this scorching hot August day, that the stumpy surfboards were once again making waves.

Everything was going swimmingly until one of the boards slipped from my son's grasp and down the shallow rapids that overlay the hairy green rocks. As it drifted downstream, my son's cries of terror perforated the air. I squeezed out of the waterfall and attempted (robotically) to wade across the pool and save it. I had no chance in that wetsuit … but as a trier, I tried. To my delight, the man, whom I had momentarily forgotten, jumped up, lunged into the water, and heroically rescued the paddle board. But as he returned the board to my son, he slipped and fell, soaking himself. Poor guy! It was not the nicest reward for a moment of uncommon gallantry. Without blushing, he preceded to remove his t-shirt and placed it beside him to dry, revealing an attractive body. Afterwards, he looked my way … 'Thank you!' I whispered warmly.

Rivers are mysterious and magical places.

Wonders continued … And soon my children began their annual search for crayfish. I don't eat fish. The children don't either, at least, not with me. Searching for crayfish was more for exploration purposes and turned out to be educational both for the children and me. Two kinds of crayfish huddle around the edges of natural pools along the River Tees: brown ones and bluish-grey ones. And the relationship between them, I would soon discover is fraught with tension. The children caught some crayfish in clear picnic tubs, goggling their features, before transferring them to a smaller pool embedded in the rocks. Soon after, they began to ask me questions to which I had no immediate answers. Good questions, such as, 'Where do they (crayfish) come from?' Luckily, the handsome man, still nearby and happily half-naked, was able to enlighten us. We learned that the crayfish had been introduced to the river as food. A statement which led my imaginative writer's brain to conclude their presence in these waters had been masterminded to satisfy the appetites of some far larger and highly ravenous water creatures. In hindsight, it wasn't a well-thought-out hypothesis. And this was confirmed by the man, who said (while laughing), he believed that the crayfish had been introduced for *human* consumption. I suppose it does makes sense. In any case, my lack of crayfish knowledge was speedily replaced by a look of disgust and mild retching; prompted by the thought of *eating* one of those slimy creatures—I don't have to love them, to respect them, or to wish them long and happy lives.

Further research on the crayfish (at a later date) would lead me to an article in the Teesdale Mercury, entitled 'Crayfish 'suck the life' out of River Tees'. Now from what I had seen earlier, they were more nippers than suckers, but the article intrigued me, nonetheless ... 'WRECKING

HAVOC: A Signal crayfish – an invasive species. It is a voracious predator, feeding on fish, frogs and invertebrates, as well as plants and even their own kind ….' Trapping and the reintroduction of Chub fish (*Squalius cephalus*) is (apparently) a way to deal with the issue. Chub had once been abundant in the Tees waters, but they had died out. Chub were a worthy suggestion, I felt, given that they are notoriously difficult to catch (a challenge to both anglers and Signals; a small but satisfying thought). Otters, however, are also effective …

Mother Nature knows her habitats best.

The day ended by the big falls further upstream—a large chest-height natural Jacuzzi—shallow enough to wade into and stand up again, if you fall over. The perfect place for children to test their wits and claim their river prowess. The man and his brood joined us. And at last, my wetsuit had stretched a bit. I showed the children how to breathe and speak behind one of the smaller waterfalls—a trick I had learned in my youth and was glad to pass on to future river generations.

Let me drink from dewy pools of rain,
Surrounded by valley flowers—
Forget-me-nots, red campions,
Wild garlic groves and lilies,
Conker paths and kissing gates,
Trees wrapped in ivy arches—
Gathered around for stories.

Peace and Presence

I am useful here. I am useful in this solitude; on this chair, on this bench, on this wooden trunk wrapped in ivy on the riverbank, and on this little patch of grass, and this little acre of sand, and by this tree, and on these smooth brown rocks.

I am useful when I am not *doing* anything. I am useful when I do not *say* anything. I am especially useful when I do not *think* anything.

I am useful when I have no spare change in my pocket. I am useful when my pen has no ink, and all the notebooks are full.

I am useful when I do not have the answers and when I do not have any questions. I am useful when I cannot predict the future or cannot remember the past.

I am useful when I cannot decide what to cook for tea. I am especially useful when the internet is down and the TV is off, and my mobile phone is in a drawer.

Fishing Signs

There are signs for fishing along rivers. Why should riverbanks be assigned to fishing only? Why aren't there signs for walking, drawing, reading, writing, making love if the mood suddenly takes you, wildlife spotting, sleeping, knitting, cloud watching, tree climbing, picnics, paddling, meditating, breathing, observing, or singing along with the blue tits?

Thankfully, nature is intelligent and has effective ways of hiding signs, such as growing great strings of ivy around and over them. A readable sign has *never* crossed my path!

Wild brown trout, grayling and the freshwater salmon, chub, prehistoric-looking perch, pike, and silver roach, are some fish that swim in the River Tees. But I cannot imagine they enjoy being hooked *for fun*. Who in their right mind would?

I suppose what I am saying is this: If I had to choose, I would sit with the canoeists—the surfers of the rivers, the wild ones in wetsuits with their well-kitted-out go-anywhere vans and steaming flasks of hot chocolate.

After-note: I talked to a lovely fisherman today. He wore a navy fleece, an empty bucket, and a sunny outlook. We joked about the thankful absence of randy cows by the riverside, and I couldn't help but like him. Perhaps they aren't all river barbarians after all!

A Forest Awakening

The forest is awake! Louder and livelier than usual. I have walked these woodland trails hundreds of times. I have jogged. I have sat silently, moved only by the spring breeze. I have meditated. I have watched the wild, black-billed geese glide across the water, from the little wooden bench by the sturdy wooden bridge and listened to their chatter as they sailed away again. I have beckoned the green mallards and brown mallards, male and female, to my feet upon the wild riverbanks.

Each season a new show; white hawthorn blossoms resilient in the light rain, daffodils and bluebells and the pink flowers of the red campion, and yellow catkins of the white willow arched over the lily ponds and gently swaying by the river.

The dusty paths know my feet. The fresh morning winds know my lungs. The trees, my faithful friends, know my secret thoughts and longings.

A young, light-footed, fawn-coated hare first crosses my path; white tail bobbing, as it hops across the uncut grass and slips beneath a maze of branches strewn across the still-damp ground.

Beautiful birdsong arrives soon after—harmonious blue tits, a fluttering joy, echoing across the sweeping canopies of oak, chestnut, and evergreens. The faint calling of the passerines looking for love … Females listening keenly for the best singer of the day—a tell-tale sign of his avian prowess. The wrens, no doubt, trying to keep the harem happy. A dawn chorus in full orchestral rapture!

Next, a trio of friendly mallards swims toward me. It may be the notable absence of other humans or the recent reduction in social stimulation, but I am certain they are speaking *directly* to me, and that I understand them … One is not content to linger and wishes to move on. Another stubbornly protests, dragging its webbed feet through the muddy water. The last (stoic throughout) shrugs its feathers and swims along, taking in the pleasant countryside views.

Further up, the grey squirrels are jumping from branch to branch and tree to tree through the canopy. They are chasing each other like our children often do at playtime or playful lovers in the climactic mists of a steaming hot summer.

I make my way up the crooked steps, along the upper edge of Quarry Wood where the path snakes around thick trunks overlooking a partially hidden green pond below. The drumming calls of the red-feathered woodpecker fills the air. So distinctive is its voice, I stop in my tracks and follow the noise to an unusually tall tree, from which it can be seen— standing at a quarter-past-three—banging its beak into the bark. It bangs a few more times and moves up. It taps again in quick succession, then moves up. And on it goes until it nears the top.

I had never observed a woodpecker going about its morning business. And I had never seen a bird with a red hat and tails!

'Hidden beneath the roots of the trees,
An underground highway of connections is laid,
And trees once thought to be mute and stiff,
Enjoy nature's internet throughout their day;
Tales of growth, of newcomers, and toils,
Stories of greedy land grabbers,
And adventurous girls and boys.

This is the great secret the sacred mother tree keeps,
As her long and nourishing limbs dive deep
And connect to a hundred trees or more;
A caring elder for those with broken branches
And those with softened bark and trunk,
And their final show of leaves …
As she passes on her ancient woodland wisdom
To future generations of seeds.'

Twang

An elegant white swan sweeps across the still waters of the River Tees. My second silent visitation in two weeks. It is a mute swan, but I won't learn this until I research it later. And I have no idea whether this elegant bobbled-beaked creature is male or female—though it matters not to me—I am content to be in its company, regardless.

It is a warm April morning. The sun is white-hot and sending out radiant rays—befitting of any magnificent star.

The swan is close, close enough to stroke … It pecks politely on the sunlit grass at my feet. 'Good morning!' I say, aware that this may be the only conversation I engage in with another heart-beating being, outside of my home, for several days.

Over the years, I have taken my daily walks and drinks of natura, as sustenance. One needs the inspiration to continue. One needs to fill up one's cup, for any hope of it spilling over and the page becoming drenched.

Writers are curious people! We are observers, questioners, investigators, imaginers, and treasurers of quiet cosy spaces. You will catch us pondering, gazing into the air and at the stars. You will find our fingers pouring over tatty cloth books, and when emerged from our creative cocoons back into society for some brief flirtations with socializing— talking passionately and diversely. Our hearts are libraries of wonder, and our minds are labyrinths of exploration.

Intuitive solitude—practised solitude—solitude that inspires the senses and sets alight a spark of genius … to be explored, serves the creative essence of a human/soul well.

This morning, the swan is the subject of my fascination. I wonder where it has made its home, along these wild banks of the River Tees. Perhaps, where the trees take their morning dip and roots sprawl, or maybe around the long curve, further up. I wonder if it has any family and any friends or if it is also estranged … The swan is content and silent, still nibbling the grass, and in no rush to move on.

Wise swan, clever swan.

This is today's river meditation.

'She walks in beauty, like the night
Of cloudless climes and starry skies;
And all that's best of dark and bright
    Meet in her aspect and her eyes;
Thus mellow'd to that tender light
    Which heaven to gaudy day denies.
One shade the more, one ray the less,
    Had half-impaired the nameless grace
Which waves in every raven tress,
    Or softly lightens o'er her face;
Where thoughts serenely sweet express,
How pure, how dear their dwelling-place ...
    A mind at peace with all below,
    A heart whose love is innocent!'

—Lord Byron

Two Writers by the Water

It is the end of June. In one solitary month alone, I have witnessed large hailstones, luminous blue sun rays, and enough rain to create an entirely new North Sea.

Yesterday was hot; 30 degrees in north-eastern England—summer holiday weather, marked by the June 21st Solstice, when the Earth (the North Pole specifically) at its fullest tilt towards the sun at 23.5 degrees, ushers in warmer months in the northern hemisphere. With maximum sun exposure and the longest day and shortest night retrospectively, barbecues appear across the land, accompanied by water-catapulting contraptions, inflatable pools, and a fearless unveiling of winter-kept skins—seizing the opportunity to be transformed into bronzed Adonises.

A happy and often unexpected advantage of being both a river frequenter and a writer who lingers for hours in the wild clutching a notebook and wandering with a mysterious gaze is that you meet like-hearted folk; wild swimmers, hikers, outdoor grazers, semi-professional skimmers, and parents who like to set their children free … A meeting place of souls-in-sync which Mother Nature, the greatest of all playground creators, is the best able to provide.

Ruth, my first (real) writer friend and I, met this way, in the sweltering sun. Following hours of writing beside beautiful waterfalls upstream, I packed away my laptop and wandered downstream to dip my legs in the shallow water. Ruth was also wandering and having mastered the art of sensing other writers, eventually came over to say hello … She, being a journalist and me—a new novelist, we bonded in a moment of professional serendipity and an unexpected but highly welcomed shared love of river dips. I discovered that journalists *can be* lovely, approachable, honest, and fun to be around. And in return, I was thrilled to be her new and ever-so-willing aquatic partner! It wasn't long until we were chest-deep in the River Tees with water swirling all around us. We soon discovered that the waterfalls I had longed to swim since childhood, were indeed incredibly fast and (in some parts) unfathomably deep!

I'll never forget that moment, while attempting to swim upstream and back to the falls … giving it my all … and realizing after tremendous effort and out of breath, I had not moved an inch! What we lacked in long-distance swimming, we made up for with pure endurance. After a few moments floating downstream, the river became shallower, and it was possible to wade toward the rocks and start again. We did this several times, and much laughter was involved. And we have enjoyed several river adventures since.

Between the trees where the falls flow freely, and swallows play in the dancing light; nature's song sings ever so sweetly, while the shadows are a shelter for blossoming life. A hand in the water renews all memories; an ancient past stored in our bones. A drink of light air, the kiss of a butterfly—the river calls all who are ready, home.

Grey Squirrels

Two silver-grey squirrels are engaging in woodland combat; hind legs stiffened, small, neat ears pricked, fast furry fists sweeping through the warm morning air. They are jiving upon an old decaying log—lit by rays of gold sunlight, in a clearing close to a pond. Moving at lightning speed, they leap from the log and give chase, circling each other like little wolves, and around another nearby tree ... defying gravity. The battle moves to the ground and finally into the bushes. I am still staring at the empty log ... and wondering what could have given them cause for disagreement on this fine June day. Perhaps one of the squirrels is defending its nuts—*noble* under any circumstances. Or maybe, the other had strayed into enemy territory. Ironic, if this is indeed the case, for having been introduced to the English countryside sometime in the 1800s, the grey squirrels are often blamed for damaging woodland and the decline of the native Red Squirrel.

Sciurus carolinensis—the grey squirrel's full name.

To my delight, the defending squirrel returns! First, it surveys the surrounding bushes, pausing and sensing ... The challenger has, for now, vanished. Back on the log, I am sure, the location of the squirrel's nutty stockpile will soon be revealed ... Instead, it defies my expectations—leaps off the log and darts up the same tree it came down from moments earlier. This time, it runs up into the leaves and returns with another squirrel; a smaller version of itself. The two squirrels move down the tree together. The victor goes first ... scanning the area. The more petite squirrel follows. As they are about to leave the clearing, the plot thickens, for the third (unwanted) squirrel comes back! It promptly gives chase to the small (desired) squirrel, and as they dart around the base of another thick trunk, are intercepted by the victor/defender, who succeeds in chasing the intruder away for good. The two remaining squirrels, finally at peace, scurry off into the forest undergrowth.

I am left wondering if the smaller squirrel was a daughter, lover, or wife? Regardless, it is good to see that the masculine heart remains strong, brave, and true within the animal kingdom, as the battle for dominance continues ...

As I leave, the woodpecker is pecking again.

A Walk in the Park

I need this natural place ...
I need these wild, green, open spaces
And wandering paths.
I need the water still and lucid like a dream
And this light in its endless streams,
And this breathless undercurrent of peace—
Here among these proud and ageing trees,
Wild daisies and bluebells sprawling at their feet,
Earth's dazzling inner kingdoms—
Exotic islands of natural beauty!
The portal-sun and its purple-hued light,
Turning into gold even the darkest forms of life.
I need this natural place.

Mountain Rivers

Nowhere demonstrates the perfection of nature's design more effortlessly than in the Lake District, England. The mountains and surrounding lands are diverse in texture and tone; rich oranges and deep browns, giddy greens, and washed whites. The lakes, rivers, and streams that flow beneath, as pure as the air above, are the beautiful blues and crystal curves that cut through the valleys and rally the rugged landscapes.

I have been a frequent visitor to the Lake District since my late teens. The draw of the water was an instinctive motivation—calling to my soul like a long-lost friend. I had walked while six months pregnant with my first child and her father beside the misty mountains, greeting sheep and walkers along the way. I had climbed the steep woodland steps to the little bridge over Aira Force and enjoyed the smiles of my children as they bathed in the abundant pools of its upper gorges. I had visited the little pencil museum in Keswick, abundant in local graphite. I had taken my oldest daughter (when she was much smaller) to visit the museum of the beloved writer, Beatrix Potter, in Bowness-on-Windermere. I had camped with my three children in a giant tent on top of a hill, near the idyllic village of Pooley Bridge—close enough for young adventurers with little legs to have a splash in the lake and to catch the steamer to Glenridding. And I had swum with my children and our friends in a lake at sunset … as the last of the sun's ray slipped beneath mounts of green and cast its diamond light upon the waters. But I had never climbed a *real* mountain …

Sometimes it is not the biggest mountain you climb that brings you the most joy, but the one with the most interesting terrain and beautiful views.

Mountain trekking requires additional planning and preparation in comparison to the usual morning ramble. Unpredictable weather and terrain can be challenging. An outdoorsy friend who has memorized parts of the Lake District like the back of their hand is advantageous. Fortunately, I had befriended such a woman! To a mountain trekking newcomer, such a friend is like a golden torch shining down upon a new land of elemental treasures. Cora hikes as if the mountains are in her bones, and she was raised around them. This is not too far from the truth—think snow-covered mountain climbs as a child supervised by a knowledgeable, fresh-air loving, father-guide. Such a wealth of expertise, gained over many years and passed down through generations, far surpasses a pocket guidebook any day. Of course, it also helps if both you and your guide share a healthy tendency for intrepid exploration and spontaneous wild swimming!

Castle Crag is a jewel of the Lakes. It sits majestically in the heart of the Borrowdale Valley, at the southern edge of Derwentwater. From the ground, it has the appearance of a lushly forested ancient mountain. The short walk from the roadside parking bay to the foot of the mountain (where the waters of babbling Broadslack Gill and the Derwent River meet) provides the first glimpses of why Lakeland is so beloved by many. From Dalt Quarry, the climb and mild scramble take you up steep inclines along near-invisible paths through a sizeable mound of slate scree, towards an open-air sculpture park laden with towering stone art created by hikers, near the summit. The view from here overlooks the Borrowdale Fells; a picture of perfect natural beauty, with rolling green hills, a few valley dwellings, vertical woodlands, and the curvaceous ice-cold waters (as we would soon discover) of the River Derwent below.

One can never be sure what one will encounter when climbing a mountain. Poodle-sitting is unexpected. As is a professional photo shoot for a funeral business. The white woollen sheep wandering next to a hand-erected stone table was surreal, as well.

The two poodle dogs that briefly made our acquaintance were far stronger than they looked. Visions of being dragged from the mountain's edge (as one of them gave chase after the drone flying around and taking the owner's photographs), lingered momentarily. To my great relief, our mountain climb *did not* end in tragedy, and after a moderate wait we handed the canines back ...

Keen to test my artistic abilities, I rummaged around for ideal materials; a modest stone piece was collectively made by my friend and I and added to the mountain gallery; a slab of mouldy slate now sits vertically, wedged by smaller slates, among a small sea of others.

Heart-bursting awe came a little further on and up, at Castle Crag's peak ... Deeply rooted trees, panoramic Lakes viewing, small (perfect for wild camping) platforms, and giant stones to sit upon. As we gazed out from the summit, I was surprised to see a small boy bouncing up to the top of the mountain with his father, before paying homage to the legendary fell walker, Alfred Wainwright. Triumphant and barely breathless, this little boy's sheer determination was a joy to witness. Inspired by the child, I took a few deep breaths, but I could not escape the rosiness in my cheeks or the tenderness in my thighs.

The views of Lakeland from Castle Crag are breathtaking! The volcanic and glacial beginnings of the Borrowdale Valley (dating back to the Ordovician period, part of the Palaeozoic era, some 440 million years ago) are characterised by the deeply sculpted shapes of the landscape. The rich depths of Derwentwater and the colourful silhouettes of the town of Keswick are below, while beyond are the high-reaching peaks of Skiddaw and Blencathra. The bright sun is but an arm's reach away. The short yet intense climb had been worth every step.

Upon choosing a suitable descent, I was asked to decide between an easier decline or the loose slate option … With a vested interest in maximum thrills, I chose the latter—an almost vertical, non-existent path, with nothing to hold on to. To my great relief, I slipped only once, making a slow yet surprisingly graceful, brief stop on my bottom. I continued undeterred (minus the previous chattering) with far greater focus. My experienced friend, whose tort calves had hardly flinched under pressure, appeared light-footed as she led the way, and I was convinced she had previously had an incarnation as a mountain deer or gazelle … We trundled down through the wooded and mossier lower sections of the mountainside and headed towards the clear-flowing waters of the Derwent River.

Along the way was an inviting walk-through cave … Named after the inspiring and gentlemanly 'Professor of Adventure', Millican Dalton (1867-1947), the split-level cave was his preferred close-to-nature home during the summer months. A mountain guide and experimental designer of hiking clothing, Millican is fondly remembered for his devotion to living an outdoors life, for his campfires and camping excursions, and for being one of the first men to teach wilderness skills to women. His unpublished memoir titled, 'A Philosophy of Life'—a journal of his fifty years in the wild, and discovered at his bedside after his passing, is *sadly* still missing. In an earlier *Sunday Chronicle* interview, he had shared …

'Well, I don't sleep much, and while I am awake, I lie and listen and think. There's a lot to think about just now, isn't there? All the sounds of the nights, the roar of the mountain stream, the barking of our dogs and foxes, the cries of birds, how can I be lonely with such company?'

The River Derwent—as limpid as glass and cupped by trees either side, was inviting. Excited at the prospect of a swim and suitably clothed, I followed my friend to an idyllic riverside alcove … It was the perfect location, secluded, but not far from the main trail. To our great surprise and disappointment, as we gazed into the depths of the perfect wild swimming pool, we saw a dog lying still at the bottom. I wasn't sure if it had jumped in and died on the spot or had been lost by its owners, injured, and floated downstream. From quick observation, it had been there a while. Either way, out of respect for the dog, and put off— we moved on!

Further downstream, a few optional dipping spots were identified, with only one tiny problem—they were on the other side of the river. Luckily, I had brought my 'water shoes'. Code name for a pair of canvas trainers—soaked once and never recovered. I offered to wade across first … and in I went! For a warm day, I was not expecting the water to be *that* cold. To my delight, goosebumps had not been triggered in vain—another small alcove complete with a rope swing was waiting for us. My friend slipped off her boots and bravely waded through the chilly water and across the rocks barefooted. I stood for longer than was healthy on the riverbank with the swing in my hands, deliberating …

We picnicked beneath the mountain, enjoying nature-spirited conversation and the beautiful energy of the valley, and plotted where our adventures would take us next!

The Lakes

Wandering upon the lakeside bay,
Where trees rise forth from watery roots,
Where children come to paddle and play
And empty out their wellington boots.
Where the waves lap gently upon the shores,
And the mountain layers so glorious and green
Stretch endlessly towards the cloud-hung skies,
And each drink of air that one breathes—
Is as pure and clear as the stars on high.
Where the days are filled with untold beauty,
Where gorges rush and forces pour—
And one's foot finds hearty, pine-filled forests
And countless trails and paths to explore.

Ah, the Lakes, where nature lovers roam—
Where the days are sweeter than any I know,
Where the poets and wanderers make their home.

Wild Iris

Wild iris is growing close to the water's edge upon a small island, ringed by layers of rock. It is a trio of triangular bird-like beauties nestled among several bunches of long, narrow, green leaves. Each yellow outer petal—curled at the tip and patterned with nature's brown ink. The smaller inner folds are silken and lemon coloured. Iris is an exotic addition to the riverbanks. It complements the white oxeye daisies and the buttercups and adds contrast to the purple-loosestrife and casually hanging violet-hued tufted vetch. It *would* look out of place, were it not for a single purple orchid with its inflorescence of magenta flowers and dull spotted leaves.

Each riverbank has its arrangements of wildflower fancies: Foul lords and ladies with their poisonous red berries, and spathes that entice insects into a nectar-filled lair, were found loitering not too far from the River Tees (en route to Middleton in Teesdale) one afternoon with a bookish friend. Their eye-catching qualities, intersected by the artistic silhouettes of the dried thistles lined up in straggly rows by the water, and softened by the white blossoms hanging low across the freshly petalled paths.

Upon the outskirts of towns closer to her source, the River Tees bends into an almost endless display of wild colour and forms. Beginning early with snowdrops growing out of riverbank sand and water alike, and nearby beds of bluebells, cheerful lesser celandines and sunny primrose, slow-growing white *Anemone nemorosa*—an ancient forest keeper. Followed by the coconut-scented bright-yellow common gorse, and the occasional pair of Orange-tip butterflies mating on a rare but not altogether wild—patch of white bluebells. Not forgetting the forget-me-nots hiding behind the hazel tree stumps—roots still present underneath the decaying wood above—altruists of wisdom to those who wander near and breathe in their mystical air.

Take a summer's countryside walk, where the gentle folds of a small river float by and you may encounter great willowherb, herb-robert, and Himalayan Indian balm, meadow crane's bill, the pretty but poisonous ragwort, scented meadowsweet, and some wild chamomile flowers for a fragrant cup of tea.

Those who train their hearts in natural wonder shall forever know the rivers, forests, wildflowers, and oceans, as friends.

Gorges and Falls

I had never stayed in a wooden camping pod. Nor had I ever been wedged, hysterically, against a large rock in the middle of a fast-flowing river by the lovely bottom of an adventurous friend ... Some of life's most thrilling experiences simply cannot be planned for in advance!

The rivers of mountainous regions in England, such as the River Derwent in the Lake District—rising at Sprinkling Tarn and travelling on beneath Scafell Pike and on to Derwentwater, has some of the clearest waters. Here, the riverbanks are minty-fresh, and climbers nibbling on Kendal Mint Cake are only *one* contributing factor. A sip of the crisp mountain air can clear all troublesome thoughts for the rest of the day, or even the week ... if one inhales deeply. The walking trails are many, well-trodden but still inviting, and the ghylls are glorious.

I do love a river that knows it is a wild thing and makes no apologies for it.

Unless you have skin akin to that of a dolphin or mermaid or have mastered cold water tolerance, endurance and breathing skills, ghyll scrambling is often (due to the low temperatures of the pools) a spring or summer activity enjoyed in a skin-tight wetsuit. Shorts to be worn over one's wetsuit are recommended. Denim cut-offs crafted earlier that same morning (because you forgot to buy some)— optional. An old pair of trainers with a decent grip is essential. A gentle stretch of one's limbs to prepare you for the steep scramble up the gorge and the surprisingly athletic descent *may* be beneficial.

A group of adventure-spirited women and I marched up Stoney Croft Ghyll one day—only to slide, swim, paddle, and climb our way back down again. It was my first time joining the group and ghyll scrambling in the Lake District. Accompanied by an experienced guide, Graham, we embarked on an energetic watery adventure! One of the initial jumps had a round, narrow, opening into a deep plunge pool below ... After mastering this challenge, more scrambles and slides and daring dips ensued in quick succession, including the task of swimming under a large boulder solidly submerged about half a meter beneath the water, as our only escape. The natural chutes were many: short, long, curved, with idyllic pools to fall or jump into.

As I reached the penultimate part of the several-hour-long pursuit, my limbs were aching, my body temperature had plummeted, and my stomach was hungry. By this time, I could hardly lift my old, beat-up but faithful river drenched multiple-times trail trainers and attached legs out of the water. But there was one last challenge: shimmy between the rocks towards a hidden waterfall at the end. Under direction, I willed my feet and bottom into position on opposite rock faces. Peer encouragement and determination (a notable trait of the group) helped enormously. That, and the thought of a warm cup of tea afterwards! Having made it into the narrow cave-like cove at the end and to the secluded waterfall, I turned back and shuffled my way out.

By this time, I was sure that the adventure had ended, but our guide had a final surprise … He invited us to create human dams using our derrières, and when the accumulating force of the water was pushing against our backs, we broke ranks … Despite my heavy limbs, I slid down with relative ease. The denim cut-offs turned out to be a very good idea!

William Wordsworth, the great English romantic poet (who had frequented the little estuaries around Ullswater and the Derwent River) was born in 1770 in Cockermouth, Cumberland, on the fringes of one of England's most revered landscapes, and its largest National Park—the Lake District. One of the Lake Poets with friends, Coleridge, and Southey; Wordsworth noted in his work The Prelude:

'... *the bright blue river passed*
along the terrace of our childhood walk;
A tempting playmate whom we dearly loved.'

Secret Riverbanks

One must be careful with whom one shares one's *secret* river spots … For if word reaches too many ears, the beauty, tranquillity, solitude, and untrodden paths may become well-known. 'Well-known' is code for popular, and in riverbank speak, popular means: busy, bustling, bursting, beaten-down, bedlam, big crowds, and doggy bags hanging from trees.

One late summer's day, I headed to one of my treasured, usually quiet, writing spots. As I scooped my way around the dangling ivy and looked up, a half-nude man in shorts was wielding some sort of blower atop the riverbank. Grass and leaves rained down into my hair and upon the jagged rocks at my feet. Through the mists of pale green dust, I saw a plume of red hair. The radiant redhead moved towards me and smiled … I had forgotten that I had done that rare thing—I had shared the location of the river and one of my *secret* swimming destinations. It was an act of love. For she is a fellow river lover. Still, both she and the topless blower with his dramatic riverbank effects were an unexpected sighting …

The afternoon that followed was what true adventurers dream of—spontaneous, full of wild abandon, heart-opening laughter, sitting under and sliding down waterfalls, clawing oneself around the river, and rock climbing. A day made lovelier when her adoring husband and water-ready sons joined us.

That same day, my friend thanked me for sharing the river with her. They had arrived early, complete with portable fire pit which they had constructed on rocks to cook breakfast … genius! And for a little while they'd had the wild of the river all to themselves.

Sharing with souls who have similar loves and are appreciative, can be a beautiful experience.

Synchronicity: that wonderful thing that happens, when divine intelligence collaborates with our higher consciousness to manifest a magical and meaningful day!

When we are young, we live to enjoy ... We have confidence in where our feet are taking us ... And remember the footpaths and delves in the rocks that fit our feet. We *know* the way. We memorise it without taking notes. We *sense* ... We navigate. And when it rains ... we get wet, or we *wait*. Tumbles or slips do not deter us from the natural joys that are ours to claim. We fall, and we heal, and we *return* ... We wake up at the first sign of dawn because the excitement in our stomach wills us. We head out to explore and find our next adventure. This is what the wild teaches our inner child—instinct, resilience, trust, perseverance, and the rewards of playful spirit, set free ...

River Terms

Eddies—areas/places (often behind boulders and rocks) where the river naturally flows against the direction of its main currents, often in a circular or whirlpool motion.

Eddy lines—edges of an eddy, where two opposing currents of the river meet. The eddy lines are often rougher in terms of force than the eddy itself, which in comparison may appear calm at its centre.

Whirlpools—marked by eddy lines are the result of eddies, where conflicting currents push against each other resulting in the river's water being pushed down, creating a suction force.

Sentient Beings

It is a warm September morning. I am following a pair of white swans upstream along the River Tees, by the park's woodland. Their brood, now only eight to my count—a reduction of one since the last time I saw them, are resting with their beaks tucked into a white underbelly of feathers and delicate layers of warm grey.

A youngster, nearest to me, stretches out its wing revealing four layers of cascading plumage with whitened ends; a sign that these young cygnets are maturing. Their white feathered parents are watching close by, having guarded them devotedly since their birth.

I am standing on a wooden jetty—an ideal viewing platform—attempting to gain a closer-than-usual view of one of the park's wildlife attractions. I step slowly ... Two signets are lying on the slope half-submerged in the river, and are watching me sleepily … I move closer … But still, they do not rise. I sense they perceive I will do them no harm. I imagine them as proficient readers of energy, and that our previous friendly encounters have been noted. But I am never foolish enough to assume I am family. I do not have enough feathers, presently. And I've never had a particularly long neck.

I am close now—*very* close.

I think back to the rustic farm life that formed part of my later childhood years. And to the beautiful old mill sandstones and granary, and the large gardens and orchard, and the views of the ocean far away in the distance. My stepfather was an agricultural farmer. Combine harvester rides were not uncommon. I would sit on the grain mounds in the barn and try to save all the baby mice that accidentally got sucked up from the fields and spat out again. I'd make their rescue houses from cardboard, and (unwisely) offer them cheese from the fridge. I still remember the smell of the soot in the fields after harvest time, and barbecues in the snow, wearing snowsuits. And the joy of having a hand-built adventure assault course in the garden. And my pet goat with the floppy ear, and the little lamb we fed with a bottle named Willy! And the wild polecat that came to stay in the wheelhouse one winter. And the pony rides in the paddocks, and the regular, around the bonfire, biker rallies on our lawn. But I could never stomach the sight of pheasant strung up outside. I wanted to set them free …

Fending off hissing geese after breakfast or upon returning from school was a routine task. The old gander was grumpy. My younger brother, John, had a superpower of sorts when it came to gander management; as a toddler, he would sit among them, and they would gather around to protect him! Goose-whispering is an uncommon skill, I believe. And clearly not one that I inherited. I stood my ground, but if I made a run for it, that old grumpy gander would give chase … This is how I became good at high jumping over sandstone walls!

Swans, though related to geese, have proved themselves more peaceful beings. And seem, as far as I can tell, to like me far more. No hissing. Instead, 'Huh huh huh huh …' translated, *I think*, as 'Necks-up! Humans are here …' Today, and despite being within arm's reach, they hadn't murmured. After a minute or so, the two that were watching me tucked themselves into their feathers and closed their eyes.

The caring of the young that can be observed in wild animals, and their desire to both protect themselves and their offspring from harm supports the observation they are sentient.

The water is as sleepy as the swans—gentle ripples reflecting the warm sun and silence. I've been here nearly an hour already; enough to ground these beautiful early-rise energies and fill my lungs with soft light air.

'I've never seen them so peaceful,' says a male canoeist arriving at the scene. The canoeist lives in a local town and visits here often. We talk about our love of rivers and their beauty and tranquillity, and the benefits of being in nature during unique times and the digital age. We enthuse over our shared love of waterfalls, and I listen keenly to his knowledge of canoeing around falls and rivers, and those he has visited in the Yorkshire Dales. Soon afterwards, another canoeist joins us at the jetty—a lady with warm, 'Good mornings!'. Arriving from the river, she paddles towards us. The male canoeist greets her like an old friend, and asks, 'How is the water today?'

River-folk love meeting other river-folk.

A dog full of adventure, suddenly runs onto the jetty. The parent swans sense him and arise, and in a single swoop of feathers, launch themselves into the water—swiftly followed by their children!

Sometimes, I have to walk—
I have to move away from the bricks
And the noise …
And let the sky unfold,
And the doves flutter beside me,
And the raindrops splash,
And the leaves blow wildly.

Acorn Rain

In September the forests rain with acorns. Sounds of pattering and crunching echo through the trees, as each fruit breaks from its ranks and tumbles to the Earth. An acorn's destiny is partly determined by the winds and rains, by wildlife, and feet—large, small, and furry. Who decides, I wonder, which seeds will grow? And does the great Mother—nature, oversee those whose time of new life has arrived?

A year of the oak's cyclical life is contained inside its hard-helmeted offspring. From its bare branches of winter to its first yellow show of pollen-generating catkins, to the lush green layers of deep-lobed leaves bursting forth with wings from their buds, and the rust—the gold before the mahogany red, and *finally* the release—the tiny oaks holding the sacred wisdom of their ancestors—carrying the foundations for wise woodlands of the future.

Stand still below the broad-crowned oaks and the acorns will shower around you. Some will bounce upon the woodland floor like balls. Some will lose their hats. Others will roll down hills with glee.

Close your eyes and listen; for you are caught beneath a mystical rain cloud with nature spirits dancing all around you.

Note: This exercise is not to be attempted with the conker (horse chestnut) tree unless wearing protective headgear!

Where Poets Wander

In all my years of wild swimming, paddling, writing and otherwise basking beside waters, the River Ure and its series of falls in the quaint village of Aysgarth in Wensleydale, England are some of the most beautiful waters that I have visited.

The old English romantic painter William Turner once painted Aysgarth Force (as it was earlier known), after reportedly visiting the area in 1816. Turner's depiction is a soft and tumbling waterfalls series travelling through a high and rocky valley, with two men on the riverbank.

From Freeholders' Wood and nature reserve and along the tree-lined paths leading down to the riverside, sounds of the water call ... The closer one gets, the louder the roar of the river and the greater the swirling sensation in the pit one's stomach. The Ure is wide with five prehistoric boulders placed at her centre: sculptures in a water park. To the right, upstream, a half-canyon sits around 6 ft (1.83 meters) high—seven adjoining falls in a row, tumbling over layers of dark rock. *This* is the introductory layer of Aysgarth Upper Falls.

Forming part of the Yorkshire Dales National Park, the carboniferous limestone rocks of the riverbanks show signs of ancient weathering and have a smooth, porous, quality. Small potholes are dotted among its homely curves.

To my left, a giant chunk of rock and earth hangs— a 15-inch gap (at least) beneath. It looks like the head and mouth of a giant earth turtle—a mythological beast of old, with trees and yellow wildflowers and bushes growing out from the top of its head—arriving at the falls, no doubt, after a long and arduous journey for a well-deserved drink. And what better place for rest than here?

All the world is quiet—except for the rush—the constant surge of the river and the endless flow of liquid light slipping from pool to pool.

'Wow!' … I say repeatedly, not caring who may hear me. It is a moderately challenging climb down and a small jump, to escape the beaten path and crowds above. At the water's edge, you can taste the precipitation, you can sense the vibrations of the currents, and inhale the freshness. Down here, bodily cells spring to life and call your heart to attention.

Exploration comes first … Better to walk a little and become acquainted before taking a dip. As a first-timer, I am still learning where the deep bits, slippery bits and fast bits are … Finding out is part of the fun, even if one needs to tread consciously.

Hidden below the water's surface is the thick, green, moss carpet I am familiar with. Walk on this and you will not slip—*most of the time.* Not to be confused with the slimy thin algae that ooze over rocks, spreads in warm weather and is *exceptionally* treacherous. River carpet has the texture of a hairy sponge … and is useful (due to its more rugged consistency) when edging one's feet through shallow currents.

A few steps downstream and across the smooth, warm, holey rocks, I sense there is more to see … To my delight, I soon discover a second lower step of falls, more beautiful than the first. After climbing down and over elegant streams, I find myself front row … It is better than

I had imagined. It is perfect. I have wandered into a waterfall paradise!

Words cannot always convey the depths of pure awe one feels in places such as this; where for millions of years, Mother Earth's beauty still flows untarnished.

Many have come here today, to be by the water's edge. Some are eating picnics and paddling further upstream. Young, middle-aged, and older; the river has no age limit. Everyone looks happy—even the dogs!

I cannot wait any longer ...

I head back to the alcove along the riverbank where my bag is hidden, and my eldest daughter is exploring the rock pools ... It warms my soul to see any of my children enjoying natural wonders, especially as they grow, and when life has so many worldly temptations to distract them.

I wrap a fleeced blanket around my waist and slip off my shorts and underwear, and discretely shuffle my swim skirt over my legs and bare bottom. Swim skirts are a new outdoorsy experiment for me. They allow for a wide range of movement, and if you are the adventurous sort, provide a modicum of modesty; never a bad thing when climbing and navigating rocks or mild currents.

I walk across the shallow water towards the first tier of waterfalls—the seven adjoining, and sit in the nearest for a photograph. There are only a few inches of water on the ground … Surprising, given the spread and height of the falls themselves. Though, this varies greatly on rainfall and snow levels. But the thinly layered water is moving fast … As I stand and attempt to walk away, my foot slips from beneath me … In slow motion, I fall horizontally and hit the back of my head … A man and his son wobble over immediately, and ask if I am, '… alright?' I look up and tell them that the rocks are *very* slippery. Something that was no doubt startlingly evident from my lying there. Damn slime! The swim skirt, however, had proved it was up to the challenge. Only my vulnerability was revealed temporarily. In comparison, I knew that my canvas shoes were not well-suited. More grip, next time, more grip! I thanked the kind strangers and moved on … Doubt is the enemy of any true explorer! I looked back with a smile at my two helpers risking it all for a few moments sitting in that first section of sensational waterfalls.

You can't keep a true adventurer down for long … For like springy river moss, they are surprisingly strong and stealthy and resurface in the most unlikely of places.

Afterwards, we head down to the lower section, and to the spectacular swimming and sunbathing spot, I had found earlier—where the old mill over Yore Bridge can be viewed downstream. We spend hours in the water, exploring. The falls are too beautiful for words. I climb the rockiest part and sit in the river with arms outstretched. Pure joy fills my heart. I swim to the hidden place carved like an outdoor shower—the perfect kissing spot. I stand at the base of the largest section, a two-stepped wide waterfall, waist-deep with her full force pushing against my legs. My thighs and knees are shaking, it is a challenge to stay upright in such fast currents. Her power is impressive, but I am anchored in my heart and unnerved. There is deep peace in this flow …

It is incredible how uplifting the elements are. There is an unspeakable connection in our DNA. The thunderous rush of the water silences all outside noise and at that moment it's only you and the raw energy of the earth—you and the river——unity.

Romance is in the air. *Love* has always been a wild thing!

'In spate' is an expression used to describe a river in overwhelming flow. Wild swimming is best done, when not 'in spate.'

January

Snow. Snow. Snow.

So far, this year, Earth has been cool. Snow boots and insulated coats, warm gloves, and frosted breath. A deep crunch underfoot, leaving a trail of mysterious footprints. The sledge rope breaking, withered from the year before, remade with stronger twine—two ample strings to hold the weight of a small child, clutching her hatted doll. The rosemary is wild, unattended, and overflowing. The sage is larger than life.

Ice. Ice. Ice …

The skies are clear blue, and the roads are snow laden. The country paths are quiet but not silent. It is zero degrees on the thermometer in the car. I climb out gingerly. The ground is compacted in shades of black and white. The leaves are as crisp as the air, imprinted with tales of the autumn. The cold is eased by the light of the still rising sun.

A walker clad in mismatched woollens is walking precariously toward me. I like her instantly. I observe her from the corner of my eye as I wander towards the bridge in case she falls ... The River Tees is as beautiful as I left her, though noticeably after the Christmas period, a little fuller around the edges, and a little heavier around the middle. The rocks and valley banks have risen to the occasion and are holding her in place. The woman walks towards me and begins to chat. Her woollens are more striking in proximity. Another serendipitous meeting of kindred river-loving souls. She's a local villager—a native of the countryside. And I, a paddler, swimmer, stay-all-summer adventurer, walker, and Mother Nature enthusiast for over forty years. We laugh a lot—frequently flashing our teeth. Who would have thought that a simple thing like an unobstructed smile could say so much? She invites me to explore a local group of creators and to share my writings, the name of which I do not think to write down and forget, soon after. I am grateful, nonetheless. And I suspect we will meet again.

The day is bright—it seems like summer, but every breath is frozen.

I wander along the valley banks, and weave between the ivy trees to a hidden waterfall I like to write beside; a trickle in summer when the dried lands do not feed it; an oasis in winter, after the snow has fallen heavily and covered the lofty fields in white. Streams slip underneath the trail paths and farmer fences, and make their way here into the valley, around the fairy coves, under the dense bramble arches, and through steep green descending banks of 100 ft or more. The water is jumping around with delight. It is fresh. So fresh, I wonder what it would be like if all the world were free of toxins, and the waters were pure enough to drink … Down I go—down the path (that's not a path, but where my feet readily go without instruction), to the place where the waterfall meets with the land and the River Tees, below. I am greeted by luxurious carpets of moss, and assume them to have elemental gardeners, so pristine are they kept. The words, 'Go lightly!' echo in my ears, as I walk. The water is lapping gently upon the exposed roots of the riverbanks. It is filled with the sun's rays and twinkling like stars: gold, violet, and rose. The river is wise. The trees keep her secrets … Even now, when the lands are still, they guard her.

Flattened white and frosted, the ground and grass are crisp yet cushy underfoot, aglow in the January light. My bottom, half-chilled, is perched against a thick, uprooted tree trunk around three meters wide. The trunk is partially dipped in the river, with its roots and mud still intact. The tree arches hang, a little longer than the year before, with leaves attached to ivy strings, drinking from the surface of the water. Such crystalline beauty—my pen cannot capture or convey its depth. Giant icicles hang over the narrow falls behind me. The leaves by its edges have frozen into large ice sculptures. Everything is familiar and yet everything is new. Stand still for too long and the air will smother you with frost and hold you in the landscape. Move too fast and the wonder is lost.

I stay for as long as I can bear the frost biting at my fingertips. I make notes. I take photographs. Afterwards, I leave … Asking the trees for assistance as I climb.

Back in the warmth of the car, with the engine roaring, feeling filters back into my toes, and my hands remember their grasp. I head back, with surprising warmth in my chest, for home-made apple and parsnip soup, and rosemary bread—poked with herbs foraged from my garden.

Walk with me ...
Along the forgotten paths and mud-thick trails;
Where the trees bow low and arch politely,
And the streams are filled with yesterday's rain.

Treecreepers

The high-pitched call of a little brown bird has caught my attention. I am sat on rocks, meditating, camouflaged, below a steep riverbank. The bird is climbing vertically, up thick root-like arms huddled around a nearby tree. It hasn't seen me … here, with my boots half-dipped in the water.

The bird is unusual; petite, maybe only four inches long, with a pure, white-feathered front, speckled brown wings, and a stiff tail. It is circling the tree, looking for something … and disappears.

I take a few breaths and close my eyes—ready to relax into a few minutes of serenity when I am startled by the bird's distinctive call! I look over to the tree as it returns, and forages, upright, among the bark. Berries are hidden among the leaves—the bird is seeking them out with its sharp curved beak.

Mother Nature has taught me the art of being a silent observer. I see more ... I notice the small things ...

But in truth, I'd never been much of a bird spotter, until a friend gifted my youngest daughter a set of simple wildlife and wildflower books. We often take them into the garden, and I am teaching her to look for wildflowers that grow beside rivers. A fun hobby that I hope she will carry with her as she grows. *And* when nobody is looking, I often borrow the books myself ... and take them out into the wild with me ... 'Spot 50 Garden Birds' by Miles Kelly is how I identified the treecreeper!

Perhaps with more effort, I'll advance soon.

Frisky Bullocks

Aside from the two occasions that I have sat on one, I have not had much experience with cows.

Picture this scene: I awaken at six am. I have taken my children to school; clothed, breakfasted, packed lunch boxes made, and water bottles filled; kisses and encouragement were warmly given. I head outdoors … The sun is blazing but there's a chill in the April air. Along the banks of the River Tees, birdsong and the first white flowers of the blossoming hawthorn greet me. The river is sparkling, and the shallow pebbled pools are idyllic. The wanderers that pass me by, on their homeward journey, appear to have an extra bounce in their step. Among the riverbank's islands are giant uprooted tree trunks, neat tufts of grass, and several relaxed Willow. *This* is Broken Scar—a popular stretch of the River Tees, restrained by a weir, and overlooked by Tees Cottage Pumping Station (established in 1849 as a radical move to pipe clean water to nearby residents, rather than relying on rainwater tubs and wells, and later closed in the 1980s). It is also a spot noted for its invisible undercurrents. And, because of this and if you are lucky enough, rare ice pancakes; an incredible display of Earth's artistry caused when river foam and swirling underwater meets with freezing temperatures. I was fortunate enough to encounter this beautiful phenomenon one frosty morning and to photograph them. More commonly seen in the Baltic Sea, North America and Canada, ice pancakes make an interesting and striking addition to any chilly river walk.

Today, I have taken the path closest to the water— the one where Mother Nature has torn apart any human attempts to lay concrete and alter the landscape; roots that climb out of the soil like tendons and bones, elbows, knobbly knees, that sort of thing.

The water sounds sacred, a lost language.

The first fence climb-over arrived shortly thereafter; a turnstile, and a welcomed gap between the bottom-biting barbed wire. As my foot hits the wood, I pause … On the other side is a herd of humping cows. This is the first time that I have encountered them along this trail and most definitely my only meeting with cows so randy. I'm not sure if they are running wild (having jumped a farmer's fence) or if the field ahead is their springtime garden. I have no one to ask, *except* for the cows. It had been a while since my confident cow riding days of old but with many years of farm experience, albeit mainly agricultural, I decide that I will march on discretely, dipping between the trees. I climb over the turnstile and head to the water and the farthest edge of land. As I look up, I see the cows have stopped in their tracks and are watching me … Some begin to move down from the field at the top of the path … I back away steadily, as far as I can go, until I am stood on the edge of the riverbank with a two-metre drop a toe's width away. I hold my ground, but the cows are coming closer … They are noisy—chattering to each other and mooing loudly at me! Using my limited experience of cow linguistics, I quickly determine that they are *up for it!* Thoughts are rushing through my head; I'm certain I could stand my ground against one or two—speaking firmly, as you would to a cheekier than usual child, but I count about ten of them, maybe a dozen, and others further up in the field. I have about eight seconds to make an exit plan; slide down into the water and wade out to safety (it looks reasonably shallow but cold) or make a run for it back to the turnstile. Some smaller cows at the front of the herd quicken their pace … Instinctively, I run … A fifteen-meter sprint (roughly). I *must* win the race … Or else they'll block the way out and I'll end up in the river! I leap through the turnstile to the sound of hooves pounding behind me and stand panting on the other side of the fence. My heart is thumping in my chest! I have always been decent at short runs. If it had been a longer distance or I'd been a child or had a disability, or a much older and less nimble walker … Who knows? The cows have huddled together on the other side of the barbed wire—an arm's length away. Some are still watching me. One is still happily humping. *I suppose* it is a pleasant enough day for it.

I study the cows. They seem excitable and youthful. They have peeking-through-horns, tags, and dark furry coats. Definitely bullocks! But this wasn't clear from a distance. They are bigger when in proximity or stood on their hind legs.

I am about to turn back and give up when a friendly female walker approaches … She has been walking this trail—a circular loop of several miles, for many years. She informs me that the field ahead, through which cuts our rights of way, *is* used by the local farmer for cattle grazing during warmer months. The woman is convinced that the bullocks, having been cooped-up for many months over winter, would be *extremely* delighted to be set free. I empathise with the cows. And, after a short conversation, I ask the lady, who seems unnerved and suitably bullock-skilled, if I can walk alongside her for a while. She kindly agrees, and we climb over the fence and continue chatting. And for a moment I feel a molecule of safety *until* a man and his three border collies hurries towards us from the opposite direction. The bullocks are now chasing his dogs! Thrown together in an unusually risky situation, the woman walker says her goodbyes and disappears quicker than mist. Meanwhile, the remaining herd is heading for the newly formed quintet; the man, his three dogs, and I. We are surrounded! The man motions me to stand behind him, for safety. And once again the cows move closer ... This time jogging. 'We'll have to make a run for it ...' I say, feeling foolishly knowledgeable. We run ... But as we reach the fence, I feel a wave of panic—the cows are almost blocking the turnstile and the barbed wire looks uninviting. In a moment of chivalry, the man has a short stand-off with the bullocks—wielding his hands like a professional herder—allowing me safe passage. Once I am safely on the other side, he jumps over the fence with his three dogs intact, behind him. We both take a few moments to catch our breath. I have no intention of a third attempt—some risks are not worth taking.

The man, whose name I soon discover to be Paul, walks with me, away from the scene, talking and laughing, and looking back at the cows in disbelief. Another man with a small dog (not his own, apparently), after hearing our tale also turns back, declaring that his wife would not like it!

I am saddened to learn that death-by-cow has occasionally occurred from similar encounters … If Paul had been present, perhaps it would have been a different story; he's the sort of man that any female walker, or otherwise, would be glad to have around in a cow crisis. And with the realisation that others had not been so lucky, I thank him for saving my life, before heading off to catch a glimpse of the plump short-tailed water-walking Dippers (*Cinclus cinclus*).

Swans, birds, and now bullocks … Perhaps the meditations are having an effect that I hadn't anticipated. Something to bear in mind, as I write by the water, and the crayfish are once again on the loose!

Farmer guidelines for cows in fields with rights of way, go something (paraphrasing, with my notes added in italic) like this:

*Try to avoid cows in fields, if possible, when they have young calves and will be instinctively more protective. *All very well, but if you head up a path, and can't see they are roaming freely, until you have wandered far from a turnstile, or they are completely blocking the path onward, what is one to do?*

*If you have dogs, keep them on leads near cows, but if the cows come close, take dogs off their leads, and the cows will chase the dogs rather than their owners. *This was only partially true, today.*

*Stick to the paths, where possible. *It is clear, this isn't always possible, as mentioned above if said cows are chasing you along the paths or are blocking the paths entirely. In these cases, one must escape by any means necessary!*

*Bullocks can be frisky when let out after winter … *During early springtime, therefore, walkers should be extra vigilant!*

Whether walkers have a right to be safe on publicly accessible paths, and/or where this responsibility lies, is a hotly debated topic! Though, as cows are used as commodities by humans, I am not sure, realistically, how much collaboration we can expect from them. Would you trust a race of beings that tore your family apart, stole the milk from your breast, and kept you in a cage?

Ramblers, the English charity, having advocated for walkers' safety at numerous farmer meetings, support walkers' rights unflinchingly. They provided sound advice:

> *If a walker has taken all *reasonable* steps to avoid the cows, the right of way would be deemed unsafe and inaccessible.

> *Farmers have a duty of care to ensure that any cattle that could be dangerous are not placed in public places.

> *Reports can be made to the local highway authority. This helps to keep the paths safe for walkers of *all* abilities.

> *Walkers' rights of way are always protected, and the paths cannot be shut off. Farmers, however,

may be innocently unaware that the livestock is causing issues, and once informed may decide *at their discretion* to place temporary electric fences or move the cows to a different field.

And on rights of way, generally:

*There are over 140,000 miles (225,308.16 km) of public rights of way in England and Wales alone, some are paths that have been used for thousands of years. In addition, the 'right to roam' or 'access land' includes mountains and moors and heaths and downs privately owned (a startling thought) and *some* coastal paths—local authority registered and managed. With exemptions on private dwellings, gardens, quarries, crop growing fields and the like.

*Official maps—*definitive maps*, have most but not all rights of way listed.

*In addition to pathways, the public has a 'right to use' bridleways and (non-restricted) byways.

Adventure assumes that life has an element of risk.
Safety asserts life's risks should be avoided.
Consciousness knows perception is important.
Sovereignty declares freedom of choice is precious!

Arctic Wildflowers

Blue is one of the rarest colours of the natural world.

Flowers serve as wonderful holders of attention for deep contemplation. For everything a flower needs to blossom and embody its signature beauty is stuffed into the tiny cells of its seed—a divine blueprint. *But it is the environment that will both shape and determine whether the flower reaches its full potential* … Too much stress too soon in its life; cold, excess water, and not enough light or love … may cause trauma and hinder the tiny shoots before they have matured. Poor soil quality and the flower's roots will lack the basic nourishment and nutrients required to grow strong and truly thrive. Too much disturbance and uprooting can create stress and shock requiring periods of recovery: Rosa, Magnolia, Cystisus, Cistus (known for honey-like essential oils), are flowers that enjoy the comforts of their well-earned root establishment, and like a woman with a freshly brewed pot of herbal tea and an enjoyable book, or perhaps a man tinkering in his workshop—prefer to be undisturbed for long periods during the maturation process.

A flower's life like a human's life, blossoms well, through balance.

Some flowers and humans for that matter, take great pride in flowering where others would shiver at the mere thought, proving that not only do environments shape us; the genetics of a species can also evolve, adapt, survive, ultimately thrive, and transcend previously perceived limitations, even within extreme conditions. Introducing arctic wildflowers—some of the wildest of the wild-flowering folk, and because of their challenging environments, also some of the most unique. Small and compact, they are designed to retain as much heat in their elemental bodies as possible. Excellent advice for campers, hikers, and mini adventurers. But the keenest of botanists may be surprised to learn that arctic wildflowers of Canadian tundras (biomes where low warm periods result in low growing seasons, treeless stretches of land and patchy vegetation), are yogi masters (according to reports of the Canadian Museum) and use popular yoga positions to thrive …

Arctic poppies (*Papaver cornwallisense*)—enjoy heliotropism sun salutations—a receptive pose—yellow petals opened wide, to gather warmth for the seeds at its centre.

One-flowered locoweed *(Oxytropis arctobia)*—prefers the child pose—huddled, compact, and positioned between mounds of rock and earth—naturally minimising its exposure to the harsh cold environment.

Black spruce *(Picea mariana)*, stands in the tree pose—holding tight—resilient, in chilling winds, along the Coppermine River valley in Nunavut; a place where wolves and grizzlies, caribou and muskoxen, roam and drink, and where lies the ancestral home to the ingenious Inuit peoples (descendants of the ancient Thule) with their small coherent sustainable communities, and gifted throat singers.

It is interesting to note that ancient cultures, along with many indigenous peoples including my own Polynesian/Samoan ancestry, have long been cultivating masterful and simple skills for living sustainably …

*along riverbanks, traversing the seas by the stars,
growing and locally sourcing food, boat and shelter
building, fire making, crafting clothes made from hand-
printed fabrics adorning patterns of beauty and meaning;
passing down knowledge to younger generations through
stories and song and tradition—real wisdom and real
life skills, in spiritual harmony with the natural world
and Mother Earth.*

For far from the icy regions of the poles or the white beaches and tropical falls of the South Pacific, is the North Pennines, in England. It is here, local legend says, live the Teesdale Assemblage; an infamous collection of rare arctic flowers; Teesdale Violet *(blue Viola rupestris)*, Mountain Pansy *(Viola lutea)*, Bird's Eye Primrose *(Pritua farniosa)*, Spring Gentian *(Gentiana verna)*, Mountain Avens *(Dryas octopetala)*, among others.

I arrive upon the North Pennines, at the small parking bay for Cow Green Reservoir, after an hour's drive up through Middleton in Teesdale and past Low Force and High Force. It is an ideal hiking day; fifteen degrees with a slight wind and warm sun shining down from a perfect blue sporadically clouded sky. The road along the reservoir has wonderful open views.

Deep stillness and beauty saturate the starkness.

The land is covered by low-lying sprawling heather, tufts of pale grass, and sheep-nibbled verges. The reservoir has the mood of a large natural lake until the concrete-slabbed wall at its south-western edge comes into view. I am heading in that direction with gusto; backpack on my shoulders and old camera around my neck, along the *Open Path* … towards the dam. It is a two-mile walk along the reservoir, approximately. In this elevated air, every step is freedom. As I wander, I begin my earnest search for that revered collection of alpine wildflowers. I spot, here and there, other wilderness enthusiasts—flora and fauna lovers—stopping and crouching and seeking … Rarest of the assemblage is the blue spring gentian—*Gentiana verna*. I am looking for her … All I see are small carpets of *Viola lutea*—purple, purple-white, and purple-yellow. But no sign of the elusive *Gentiana*. I photograph every wildflower that I come across, just in case. Mountain pansies are dotted around in small and compact communities, shining their shades of violet elemental light, in an environment that is too extreme for many. I admire them. I am about to give up my search for the spectacular, when my soul fires up—*I think* I have found two members of the assemblage:

Potentilla crantzii (Alpine cinquefoil)—An erect perennial with yellow flowers made of wide-spaced heart-shaped petals.

Polygama amarelle—A pale blue (at my encounter) flower with uprising white inner tubes of petals that have a wavy edge, and smooth green oval leaves.

But wildflowers weren't the only thing on my mind as I set off this morning, I came to finish this book …

I'm sat atop England's biggest waterfall, Cauldron Snout. Green mould has bleached the giant boulders around me. I am close enough to be mesmerised by the sheer force of the cascading water spraying my face; far enough away, that the riotous droplets of the ricocheting river have not the mass to douse my notebook as I write. Cauldron Snout could best be described as a long and deep gorge. It is a canyon cut through Whin Sill dolerite with vertical craggy outcrops on either side … *These* are the first spectacular riverbanks of the River Tees. Around the falls, sit flat-topped fells—distinctive, due to the horizontal layers of limestone and shale from which they are formed, and some 330-million-year-old air-dried tropical mud turned grey rock embedded with coral—leftover from the Carboniferous period. Sand once washed in here too from rivers of old ... preserved for our imaginings in layers of sedimentary sandstone.

My eyes follow the jet-black jagged rocks down the gorge. Heather is dotted between the boulders mottled white, also cascading in layers towards the valley below. Visitors, though relatively few in comparison to the more popular falls of High and Low Force, are wandering down and admiring the views.

The sound of natural water—gallon upon gallon—hurtling down, is one I love dearly, and yet, until this day, had not encountered in such velocity and volume. Dare I say, she is more alluring than her more popular fellow, High Force, and her beauty more striking but no less radiant because of her sheer power! As tremendous as she undeniably is, she flows effortlessly ... The white and gurgling falls slip down through the open moorland like an excited young woman, rushing to see what lies beyond ... Without realising, of course, that *she is* the main attraction. She is that which unifies both sides of the valley and nourishes them, as one. Buoyant, pure and with purposeful spirit, she moves first left, then right, and sharply left again. She plunges narrowly and suddenly—and breaks into a watery crescendo.

She is the perfect balance of the masculine and feminine forces.

I am still at the top of the falls, looking down. At the highest point, there is a sense of elevation ... I am at the peak of a great and watery mountain. All the world has disappeared. Soft, golden, creamy hues—steam clouds are rising from the whirlpools as sprays of water sprout. I am filled with reverence and peace.

Others are arriving awe-eyed with backpacks and walking sticks—with children, and solo. Cameras are snapping enthusiastically. Pure joy is palpable in the air!

This is the wonder of riverbanks, epitomised. *This* is the primal draw of the wilderness. And the deep knowing within our bodies that inspires us to seek out the inner nature of our being; a spiritual pilgrimage that leads us back into the divine temples of our hearts and souls.

After a long sit, writing, I move further down. There is no path, as such. Instead, a plunging scramble ... A mindful foot here and clever grab of the enormous rocks there, and the occasional branch to hold, while looking for any hint of a trail left behind by the locals—identifiable by tufts of deposited wool and black droppings. Sheep graze vertically, dotted along on the craggy valley banks, behind. The grass is neat—what one would expect upon moorland, with plentiful, non-horizontally challenged, lawnmowers. Smoother than usual rock faces indicate where the feet of other adventurers have also dared to venture. After a steep descent and some nimble weaving and jumping, I finally arrive at the bottom of the falls … And what a grand and beautiful greeting awaits! A wide curtain of water is stretched over dark, smooth, shining rocks with a small pool beneath.

I sit and I listen …

It is heavenly here. I close my eyes—absorbing and anchoring the beautiful aqua-sun rays. I place my hands upon my heart. I submerge them into the waters … I am giving back; I am sending my love. I sense the ancestors by my side and the starlight of my soul, offering direction for this healing of the Earth. I thank the great Mother for all that she has given me … and for all that, she has given *us*.

I see myself reflected in radiant blue-hued spherical light upon the face of the river. I sense the presence of home.

'Water is the mother of life, while also being the energy for life ... Water is the mirror of the soul ... Water exposed to the words "Thank you" formed beautiful geometric crystals, no matter what language ...'

— *Dr Masaru Emoto*

I think of Dr. Emoto's pioneering work and research into water and consciousness. And, of the beautiful imagery when samples were taken from pure sources such as mountains or were blessed or exposed to tranquil music. I think of the contrasting images—dark and distorted by toxicity in various forms. I think of the melodies of nature and their uplifting frequencies, and how natural environments act as complex sound baths for the senses. I imagine what would happen if everyone knew the mystical power of thoughts and intentions. I visualise all the conscious and earth-cherishing souls of humanity putting their hands collectively into fresh waters ... Sending love to our Earth Mother and her elements ... Millions of souls healing the rivers, lakes, and lands with the sheer power of the body's largest magnetic generator of energy—the heart. I imagine humanity as an ocean of individual water crystals transformed into shining fractals. For if we are mostly made of water, do we not also have this potential? I think about every time a child splashes happily through a stream, and each time a person swims in a river and exudes sheer beingness, and the positive patterns of crystalline ripples this could create.

At the foot of these magnificent falls and the water but a breath away, I am deeply humbled and emotional ... There are some moments and experiences in life that turn out to be more wondrous than you could ever have imagined. I still feel the energies of the rivers in my bones and the winds as my breath. But the connection has deepened, and my awareness has broadened. I understand with greater clarity and intimacy the radiance of the mother light embodied in the heart of Earth ... For she has been the greatest story, untold. *She is* the lands that shelter us. It is her fruit, that which comes from her breast, that feeds our bodies. She *is* the motherland of old. Ancient stories of Lemuria (home to my Polynesian ancestors) revered this sacred feminine wisdom. They understood the mother as one of the creator forces; the pure electrical power and energetic architecture of the father (masculine) god, and the pure magnetic power and creation made manifest of the mother goddess, as one. *She* is the living intelligence in the waters—the physical matter of the world and the substance of every soul. She is *the* great mother. *She* is why I am here ... Her truth is my truth. And this wisdom is offered to all those who come with pure and devoted hearts to her ravishing riverbanks and seek her there ...

I am profoundly changed by this journey. For when I set pen to paper to write this book, to share my love of wild riverbanks with other nature-loving souls, such as yourself, I did not realize that each part would bring into greater focus my own personal and spiritual journey. I see the deeper significance of my being here, at the start of the River Tees, waters that have been with me my entire life— writing this final chapter. The mirroring of endings, reflection, understanding, and new beginnings. Being here is no coincidence. I had been searching for this moment of revelation ... And like all good stories and adventures, the most enlightening part had been hidden in plain sight, only to be revealed at the end ...

'This is the old channel of the River Tees dating back to before the last glacial period. Debris, mainly boulder clay dumped by the ice, plugged the old valley to such an extent that when the ice melted, and the river began to flow again ...

it was diverted to where it cut a channel through the hard Whin Sill dolerite forming the waterfall of Cauldron Snout.'

— *Explore the North Pennines*

It had finally dawned on me—the River Tees is hundreds of millions of years old! The pre-glacial river channel is right in front of me. She is *truly* ancient! And like all things that are ancient and wise and strong, when faced with adversity, she forged a new path and carried on ... Throughout all my years of wandering, exploring, and adventuring along her wondrous riverbanks, for every molecule of sweat and every cup of tears, every ounce of longing, and hour of wondering ... *She* has been my greatest teacher and companion.

I have always known this, *somehow.*

You have been trodden on and ignored,
Caged, ravaged, and left raw—
But your beauty still flows
Like an infinite river,
Giving birth, through joy, rapturous streams
And multi-scented wildflower dreams.
I know who you are …
Sweet Goddess of Earth.

—Unbound

A Few Final Thoughts ...

When we set off with our backpacks hanging from our shoulders and our hiking boots unwashed from the last trail, boxes of thrown-together snacks and no map ... we never know how it will all pan out. But something deep inside calls us to adventure and to brave the unknown ... There is a bit of wilderness within all of us; soils and rocks, waters, and wildflowers, and even the stars—they whisper to us wherever we go. And the journeys we take to rediscover this, help our souls to flourish and grow ...

And having left the ordinary world and ventured further than we have gone before, and encountered that which we had never encountered, and surmounted that which previously seemed impossible ... we are changed.

We are all heroes on our unique journeys. And once committed, many helpers and unlikely companions miraculously appear; other wilderness lovers who walk with us for some of the way or offer a warm hand as we surmount slippery falls or hills (thank you, Cora) or stimulating conversation (thank you, Ann, without an 'e') or shared photography interests (thank you, Bjorn) or an unexpected ride (thank you, Christine!) or crayfish corrections (thank you handsome man!) or brave bullock defence (thank you, Paul), and countless others whose names I did not catch, but who had my warm appreciation at that moment.

And there are times when the adventure seems too difficult to continue … when one's heart is aching, and one's legs are tired, and the third-degree blisters are searing, and one's motivations are temporarily forgotten. And sometimes it is necessary to stop, take off our boots, put down the backpack and have a well-earned rest, or revisit our map and change course … But whether we have journeyed to the farthest edges of the Earth or the deepest dimensions of the soul; the gifts we return home with, be they handfuls of conkers or sticks, meaningful memories, enlightenment, long-awaited healing and peace, a sense of personal achievement, the gaining of fresh perspectives, the learning and sharing of new-found skills with our children, or renewed optimism in opening the windows and welcoming another day—we have gained *immeasurable* treasure from our travels.

> *Freedom has a frequency—*
> *It is joyous and light*
> *And uninhibited,*
> *For its origins are divine—*
> *An unconditional love.*

There is a higher intelligence and consciousness that animates the trees and wildflowers and waters; a *divine* creator force that flows ... The starlight that glistens on the river's surface is the same cosmic light in our bones and that birthed our souls. Waters give life to our bodies; we are not separate but one. *Be* in nature—take a moment to appreciate the sacredness of the natural world and rediscover your own. Reignite the ancient flames of this wisdom.

Mother Earth whispers for us to awaken and remember. It is time now ...

For *she* is evolving, too.

Deep within the crystal caverns of
Mother Earth,
A radiant light steadily grows,
Empowered by the hearts of every
Child, man, and woman,
And every loving and conscious soul.

Nature Meditations

Being able to feel the flow of the Earth's energy through my body, as a child, helped me to understand the profound oneness and interconnectivity that exists innately within us. Exploring and embodying this *oneness*, this dance of masculine and feminine energies has been a lifetime's journey of inner devotion. Conscious breathwork and meditation are some of the most powerful practices I have experienced. For breath *is* our life force. To become conscious of one's breathing is to learn how to become more intimate with one's soul essence. Nature provides many beautiful spaces to practise this essential skill and ancient art.

Accompanied by gentle and conscious breathing, we can work with Mother Earth's organic energies, and use them to further enhance our experiences of inner presence and peace. Earth is a multidimensional *living* being with recordable frequencies called the Schumann Resonance, discovered by, and named after the late physician Winfried Otto Schumann. Interestingly, during recent years, these frequencies have been ascending to new heights!

All things that we desire to flourish require
Love and devotion ... from flowers to gardens, to our
minds, bodies, lives, and, most notably, our hearts.

As so much of this book is intertwined with my meditative walks along rivers, I have included two here. May they serve you well upon your life's adventures, and help you to unearth your inner light, wisdom, and strengths. And, if find yourself estranged from the lands and waters that you love, meditating to the sounds of nature is a lovely way to relax at home and to bring the wild indoors. See the resources page, at the back of this book, for links to two tracks that I have personally used and enjoyed. They are entitled, 'Morning Whisper' and 'Sunny Mornings'.

Nature Meditation One:

Active Presence

It may seem counter-intuitive to be both active and present simultaneously, however, developing awareness in this way and attuning to the sensations of one's body is useful in developing higher sensory perception overall, and in learning to recognize the harmonious flow of energy within oneself and in our environment.

To begin, wander outdoors somewhere—forests, oceans, riverbanks—somewhere a bit wild. If this is your garden among the roses you have planted, now in their full glorious show, so be it! However, wilder is better … It is the difference between feeling *almost* fully relaxed (if in one's garden this will be pending upon neighbours and children running around) and the experience of being windswept by the ocean or mud-caked between endless rows of pine-scented trees—*immersed* in the raw elements, rather than a polite bystander.

Next, bring awareness to your feet as you walk—how do they feel? What *sensations* do you sense? What sounds can you hear? Are your limbs heavy or light as you focus on them? What perceptions of your physical body and how it interacts with the environment, can you gain from an observer's perspective?

Now, bring awareness slowly upwards from your feet and legs to your stomach and torso ... Notice how your whole being is moving you across the ground. And how your muscles are engaging, and your bones are supporting you. And how your heart is pumping blood around your body and warming you from within. Breathe in deeply. Observe how the air is travelling in from the natural environment into your body .... Take several deeper breaths in through the nose. Feel your chest rise and fill, hold for a few seconds, and release through the mouth.

Relax ...

Imagine nature's energies flowing through your body, uplifting, and supporting you ... Feel them circulating through your lungs. Observe the inhalation of breath and the exhalation of breath. Take deep breaths as you walk. Take deep, *conscious* breaths ... Each cell of your body is being rejuvenated as you move. Embrace the peace and organic flow of your being-state as you connect deeply to Mother Earth. With each breath your heart is opening and expanding into new dimensions of inner bliss. With each exhale release all tension, all worry, all thoughts of yesterday, and projections of tomorrow.

Finally, play with this! There is no one way to develop an active state of presence. Experiment with bringing awareness to your inner being when you are in other wild locations. Are there some that are more aligned and more beneficial or hold deeper memories for you? You will find that by doing this, you will also become more aware of environments that *do not* feel good, in comparison. Sensitivity can be a gift. Let the native joy within and your intuitive senses guide you.

Inexplicable wonderment is a state of beingness.

Nature Meditation Two:

Stillness and Presence

As the subtitle denotes, this meditation exercise will assist you in developing a practice of presence from a place of inner stillness. Many meditation teachers will say that you must quiet your mind, but from experience, I understand that sitting *still* can often be the first meditation hurdle. There are some keenly attuned (or otherwise ready for it …) folk, after a few quick meditation attempts will dissolve into the depths of themselves like ice melting in the sunlight. And there will be others, having never experienced the sanctuaries of their inner dimensions, who may be mildly uncomfortable—simply because it is unfamiliar territory! By placing our attention on the heart and attuning into our sublime divine energies within, we elevate our consciousness (vibration). This is how we expand our awareness beyond lower energetic states of mind that may otherwise attempt to convince you that sitting still for a few minutes in silence surrounded by nature's finest is a terrible idea. I have found that practising this kind of meditation is powerful. For when we are in the wilderness or beneath trees or beside water, there is a plethora of earthy sensations and sounds that act like harmonizing frequency baths, helping to attune the mind and body into states of presence and peacefulness.

To begin, find a comfortable, safe, quiet spot to relax. Trust your intuition and find somewhere that feels right for you.

Next, close your eyes. And then begin (like Meditation Exercise 1) to bring awareness to all the sounds around you—the birds tweeting and singing, the wind rushing or blowing gently, the rustling leaves and the whispering trees, the rush of the waterfall or gentle flow of the stream, the rain falling or a series of crashing ocean waves. *Feel* into these sounds ... *Feel* into these frequencies; each has a unique vibration but is also part of a greater collective; individual but also one symphony. Observe the sensations in your body as you connect to these sounds, and how they flow through you … Allow yourself to harmonize with nature … Be at one with the elements, and at peace within your own elemental body.

Breathe *naturally*.

Now breathe in a little more deeply and feel the expansion in the chest. Hold for three seconds, and release. Repeat this several times.

Relax …

Allow yourself to be at ease.

Breathe …

If your mind wanders, return your awareness to the inhalation and exhalation of your breath.

This is a moment of self-care and self-love. You are accessing the light of your divine inner presence and exploring the beauty of *being*.

Breathe … gently but consciously. Be kind and patient with yourself.

Keep focusing on your breathing … Feel the fresh earthy airflow filling your lungs and revitalizing your body. Inhale … Hold for three seconds … and release.

Now focus on the sensations of the chest and imagine your heart's energy field expanding into nature … Nature's organic energies are melding with your own, as one. With each breath, you are more relaxed and more present.

Breathe … Draw in the sun's radiant light into your cells …

Now feel into your heart and imagine a bright pure light emanating from its centre—a gentle golden glow, bathing you in warm energy—tingling through your body. Feel how beautiful this light is, *your soul's light*. Let it merge with the light pouring in through your crown.

Allow this inner light and presence to gently melt away all feelings of tension within you. Trust in the sensations that arise. Be guided by your body and intuitive wisdom.

Breathe and relax …

Imagine yourself being lovingly held by Mother Earth's crystalline heart. Give thanks …

Stay with this for as long as you are comfortable—breathing, and relaxing, and enjoying this *oneness*.

When you are ready, follow the sounds of nature and start to bring yourself back to your waking state.

Take a deep breath, exhale, and open your eyes.

Observe as you practise, that the consciousness you embody in meditation stays with you (as you) for longer periods throughout your day.

'Nature loves courage ...

You make the commitment and nature will respond to
that commitment by removing impossible obstacles.
Dream the impossible dream and the world will not
grind you under, it will lift you up ... This is what all
teachers and philosophers who really counted, who really
touched the alchemical gold, this is what they understood.
This is the shamanic dance in the waterfall. This is how
magic is done. By hurling yourself into the abyss and
discovering it's a feather bed.'

—Terence McKenna

Acknowledgements

Special thanks to my copy editor Debbie Stokoe. Much love to you Debbie for your encouragement and worthy suggestions, and for assisting me in making this book reader ready. The river walks and lunches are a beautiful bonus. Long may they continue!

Love to my sister and brother for allowing me to share some of our childhood memories, and to my beautiful children for our continued river experiences together. Such fun! I love you!

And to Ruth, Cora, and Paul, whom agreed to be lovingly featured. Treasured memories!

And finally, thanks to you ...

Yes, you, the beautiful soul that purchased this book. You have my love and deep gratitude for sharing in these humble stories and adventures. And I wish you many wonderful and memorable nature-inspired moments of your own.

References & Resources

Walkers' Rights of Way & Information (pg. 104)

www.ramblers.org.uk

River Levels (general resource)

https://riverlevels.uk/

River Tees History and Exploration (Introduction & throughout)

https://englandsnortheast.co.uk/2020/09/14/the-river-tees-viking-frontier/

https://www.geologynorth.uk/the-whin-sill/

https://www.discoveringbritain.org/activities/north-east-england/viewpoints/high-force.html

River Tees Trust (general resource)

http://teesriverstrust.org/

Woodland Trust – Ancient Woodlands, Tree Species & Wildflowers (general resource)

https://www.woodlandtrust.org.uk/

Rare Wildflowers *(pg. 109/110)*

https://teesdaleflora.home.blog/

https://www.ukwildflowers.com/Web_pages_intros_indexes/thumbnail_Zt
oA_british_index.htm

http://www.exploreteesdale.uk/downloads/SpringGentianTrail.pdf

Yorkshire Dales Geology *(pg. 83)*

https://wildernessengland.com/blog/the-fascinating-limestone-geology-of-
the-yorkshire-dales/

Canadian Wildflowers & Rivers *(pg. 109)*

https://www.nature.ca/en/explore-nature/activities/stretch-plant

https://chrs.ca/en/rivers/coppermine-river

https://arctickingdom.com/kataqjjaq-throat-singing/

Lake District Volcanic Origins *(pg. 57)*

https://www.nationalgeographic.com/science/article/ordovician

Ordovician Period *(pg. 57)*

https://www.britannica.com/science/Ordovician-Period

Crayfish Article (pg. 30)

https://www.teesdalemercury.co.uk/country-life/crayfish-suck-the-life-out-of-river-tees

Heart's Electrical Field – Institute of HeartMath (pg. 117)

https://www.heartmath.org/research/science-of-the-heart/energetic-communication/

Morning Whisper by Pedar B. Helland (pg. 127)

https://www.youtube.com/watch?v=FMrtSHAAPhM

Sunny Mornings by Pedar B. Helland (pg. 127)

https://www.youtube.com/watch?v=hlWiI4xVXKY

Notes

A space to gather your meditation insights, and other inspiration whilst reading.

The End

For more books & writings visit

www.atalinawright.com

www.ingramcontent.com/pod-product-compliance
Lightning Source LLC
Chambersburg PA
CBHW071845090426
42811CB00035B/2324/J